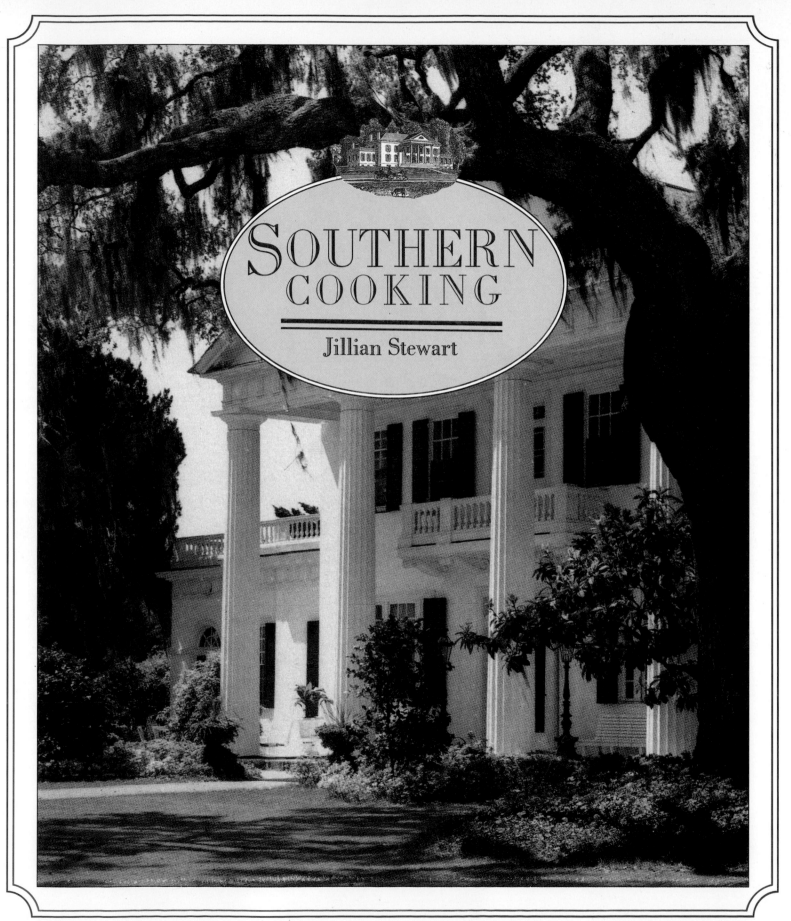

SOUTHERN COOKING

Jillian Stewart

SOUTHERN COOKING

More than 60 Authentic Recipes,
Enriched with History
and Tradition

COURAGE BOOKS

An imprint of
Running Press
Philadelphia, Pennsylvania

This edition first published in the United States
by Courage Books, an imprint of
Running Press Book Publishers.

CLB 3554
9 8 7 6 5 4 3 2 1
Digit on the right indicates the number of this
printing.

Library of Congress Cataloguing-in-Publication
Number 93-85547

ISBN 1-56138-372-4

This book was designed and produced by
CLB Publishing, Godalming, Surrey, England.

Editor: Jillian Stewart
Introduction: Bill Harris
Designers: Art of Design
Jacket Designer: Neil Hyde
Picture Researcher: Leora Kahn
Photographers: Neil Sutherland and Zeva Olebaum

Typesetting by Inforum
Printed and bound in Italy

Published by Courage Books,
an imprint of Running Press Book Publishers
125 South Twenty-second Street
Philadelphia, Pennsylvania 19103

Contents

Introduction

*Above: many plantation owners turned to antiquity for
inspiration when building their mansions, and many
feature elaborate columns, balconies and porticoes.*

Of all the varied recipes in the following pages,
from the elegant She-crab Soup and Cherries Jubilee
to the soul-satisfying Brunswick Stew and Collard
Green Soup, there is a single ingredient that sets
Southern cooking apart from nearly all the other
cuisines of America as well as of the world: the
long-standing tradition of Southern hospitality.

Since Colonial times, good food has been the
centerpiece of hospitality in the South, where people
have always instinctively treated friends and family
as well as strangers with an attitude that says, "We're
pleased you're here." And even today they never
fail to send guests away without a heartfelt, "Y'all
come back ... soon!"

Who wouldn't want to? Who wouldn't want to
come back for another slice of dry-cured country

ham or just one more piece of that memorable pecan pie? And no one could resist arriving in time for breakfast when the muffins are hot and fresh, the eggs perfectly fried and accompanied by country ham done to a sizzling turn; when the coffee is scalding hot and the fresh fruit still dripping with the morning dew ... and the whole day lies before you for quiet conversation with more good food, simply prepared and served with gracious pride.

In the 17th century, Sir William Berkeley, the Governor of Virginia, summed up the source of that pride, not just in his own colony, but for all of the South, when he noted that it was "the land of good eating, good drinking, stout men and pretty women." No travel brochure could have done a better job of luring visitors, both from the colonies of the North and from England itself. But unlike other tourist destinations, the South had few inns to accommodate visitors and travelers in those days, and they were welcomed instead to big plantation houses where there was lots of room, plenty of servants, and a strong desire to entertain lavishly. No one was more pleased by the arrangement than the host families themselves, who found visitors not only bearers of news and gossip from the world outside, but a welcome break from the isolation of plantation life.

There was plenty to impress those outsiders, but

Above: a gracious antebellum mansion reflects the elegant style of many of Georgia's historical homes.

the one thing most often mentioned in diaries and letters to the folks back home was breakfast. Breakfasts were like nothing else enjoyed anywhere else in the world, and even compared to Tudor England, which prided itself on its sumptuous breakfasts, visitors from the Old Country had to admit they had been outdone. One reason was that breakfast was part of a practiced daily routine. A typical planter usually began his day with a mint julep, "for protection against malaria," and then went out into the fields to organize the day's work, and in the process to work up an appetitite. What satisfied that appetite varied from region to region, but almost always included bacon and ham, eggs, grilled fowl and seafood, grilled meat, vegetables, hominy and corn meal mush. The fact that there were guests in the house never altered the rhythm of plantation life. Southern hospitality back then was not so much a matter of cooking for company as of sharing what the family regularly enjoyed every day of the week. The basic idea is still very much alive.

Like everything else about America, Southern cooking is a combination of all sorts of influences. It begins with colonial immigrants from Britain who arrived with their own notions of what a good meal should be. Their ideas were enriched by the native Americans, who introduced them to such local produce as sweet potatoes and corn, and showed them how to prepare it. Southern cooking picked up a French accent from Huguenots, who were among the first settlers in the Carolinas, not to mention the French immigrants who settled the Mississippi Delta, where their tradition still dominates. And it achieved a different character from slaves, who brought such staples as sesame seeds, peanuts and okra, not to mention eggplant, from Africa as part of their contribution.

Loyalty to the mother country was one of the hallmarks of the early Southern attitude, but the English looked down their noses at everything French, including the cuisine, and the colonists made it a point to follow their lead. The barrier didn't begin to come down until 1785, when the former Governor of Virginia, Thomas Jefferson, became America's Ambassador to France. While he was there, he seems to have spent more time absorbing the secrets of

French cooking than dealing with the intricacies of French politics, and when he came home he began changing the way America eats by marrying European techniques and ingredients to the already justly-famous cuisine of the South. It wasn't easy. Even his close friend, Patrick Henry, denounced him for "abjuring his native victuals." Jefferson had no such intention, of course, he just wanted to make the best better. For instance, although much of his attention was lavished on desserts, he didn't mind saying that, with the possible exception of pears, there were no fruits in the Paris markets that could hold a candle to the ones that were grown in his native South. He did, though, think there was definitely something to be desired in realm of vegetables. Although they were produced in abundance in Southern gardens, cooks were generally suspicious of them and routinely boiled them for hours to make sure any lurking poisons were destroyed. Eighteenth-century Americans also shunned tomatoes (a "native victual," like corn and potatoes, that is the New World's gift to the Old), which they believed were so poisonous that no amount of cooking could make them safe. Jefferson proved otherwise by cultivating a close ancestor of today's beefsteak tomatoes and then shocked his neighbors by eating them raw. He also introduced broccoli and endive to the local kitchen gardens, and it was his French-influenced idea to imitate the classic Gallic cassoulet, substituting black-eyed peas, creating something quite new, something quite Southern.

Not all of Jefferson's culinary gleanings were French. When he left Italy, Jefferson's pockets were bulging with rice, which he smuggled back home and introduced into the Carolinas, where it became not only the region's most important cash crop, but an important ingredient in the Southern diet.

But Jefferson's attempts at bringing Southern cuisine and agriculture into the 19th century didn't always result in culinary home runs. It is fascinating to think of the impact on local cooking he might have accomplished if the more than 500 olive trees he imported had been received with enthusiasm rather than with, as he put it, "the nonchalance of our Southern fellow citizens." What may be Mr. Jefferson's greatest accomplishment, though, was to

Above: a family enjoys one of those great Southern traditions – a leisurely meal in the shade!

convince his fellow Southerners that good food was one of life's great pleasures, and if he found inspiration abroad, his ultimate message was that the American South was a virtual Garden of Eden that needed little more than a bit of nurturing to create one of the world's great cuisines.

In his "Natural History of Virginia," written in 1737, William Byrd noted that every kind of fruit and vegetable found in Europe was grown in the Southern colonies and that the American varieties were a good deal better. After describing large, long and "splendid" asparagus and "fragrant" melons, he identified twenty-four different kinds of apple, adding that he was only considering "the best species of them." He said that the beef, veal, mutton and pork were better than the best Europe was producing (a fact Jefferson later confirmed in Paris when he promoted American meat exports to grateful European butchers). He was enthusiastic about the abundance of fish, too. "No country can boast more variety or greater plenty or better in their several kinds," he wrote. Of waterfowl, such as ducks, geese and swans, he said, "The plenty of them is incredible."

But for all the pleasure of fine dining that this new Eden could provide, most of the people who ran the large estates of Colonial Virginia were not farmers themselves and very few of them had any desire to learn the trade. It was a problem that didn't go unnoticed. Robert Beverly, who wrote a book describing the lifestyles of the rich and famous of Tidewater Virginia in 1705, took his contemporaries to account for their lack of respect for the riches nature had given them. "No seed is sown there but it thrives," he wrote, "and most plants are improved by being transplanted thither. And yet there's very little made among them, nor anything used in traffic but tobacco." After noting the folly of importing food into such an environment, he said that the men who called themselves planters "Sponge upon the blessings of a warm sun and a fruitful soil, and almost grudge the pains of gathering in the bounties of the earth. I should be ashamed to publish this slothful indolence of my countrymen, but that I hope it will rouse them out of their lethargy." It didn't work until Thomas Jefferson came along nearly a century later and began spreading the word that a man could be both a gentleman and a farmer at the same time, and Southern food took on a more respectable reputation.

But that doesn't mean that the wives of those gentlemen put on their aprons, rolled up their sleeves and went to work in front of the kitchen fireplace. Even though he knew what it took to make a great meal, even Thomas Jefferson didn't know what it took to prepare one. That was the work of slaves and servants and one only had to supervise. Lavish entertainment was only enhanced in the first half of the 19th century, when there was general prosperity in the South, and from New Orleans around and up to Williamsburg Southern hospitality reached a kind of golden age. The Civil War changed everything. Except the concept of

hospitality. If food wasn't plentiful, every effort was made to create the illusion of plenty. Even before the war, a Kentucky cookbook writer had told her readers that, "A few things well-ordered will never fail to give a greater appetite and pleasure to your guests than a crowded table badly prepared."

Although the years of Reconstruction were hard on everyone, there were many Southerners who had never experienced the groaning boards of plantation dining rooms. They had lived directly off the land all their lives, and although the war had destroyed their crops, it didn't leave them without resources. The gentry had to make some adjustments, to be sure, but simplicity had always been the basis of their cooking, and if they changed their style of life, their culinary style went through only minor changes and the marriage of the food of the frontier with the plantation tradition gave us what we call Southern cooking today.

The good news is that even in the last quarter of the 20th century, when most of what we eath as been processed beyond recognition and when many Americans think of fried chicken as a take-out food that tastes vaguely like its plastic container, Southern cooking still rings true to its roots.

Traditional southern cooking spread from the South into cities all across America, along with transplanted blacks who moved to change their lives but never lost their taste for "down home" cooking, which in its transplanted version became known as "soul food." Although its origins were in the fields and slave quarter kitchens, its basics were common to all Southern cooks, even if the style and flavor had African beginnings. Like most Southerners in the last century, black women were forced to do their best with what they had available to them and, like the pioneers who settled the West, wild greens such as collards, kale and turnip tops formed the basis of their diet. They made them palatable, even delicious, by cooking them with fat meat, whose flavor was balanced by the pungent bitterness of the greens. Apart from game, meat was scarce, but they could easily obtain, as had the slaves before them, cuts of pork that white folks, who preferred living "high off the hog," considered less than edible. In the heyday of soul food, in the 1960s, chitterlings and hog maws became

Above: cutting sugar cane in Louisiana. Like their parents, the children had to endure the hardships of plantation life.

fashionable, almost as much as spare ribs, which a century earlier had been regarded as fit only for the poor.

A few years ago, the proprietor of a New York restaurant famous for its "soul" offered this description of the style of cooking that set his menu apart: "To begin with, it is honest" he wrote. "It is easy to cook but does not adapt well to 'Let's get out of the kitchen fast' shortcuts. It is delicious food, but does not allow for any frills. Sauces, for instance, are used only because they taste good, never just to dress up a dish...It is sincere because the good cooks who traditionally prepared it always worked with their whole heart, doing the best they could with what they had on hand to make sure their dishes would be enjoyed by all who sat down to eat."

The classic definition of "soul" is best summed up as naturalness combined with openness, a sharing of both the joys and sorrows of life, and a coming together to celebrate them. The same definition applies to all of what we call Southern cooking, whether its origins are in London or Paris, the villages of the Algonquin Indians, or the slave ports of West Africa.

We live in an era when "gourmet" food is the rage. Give a can of soup a French name and its success is assured, yet good, homemade soup is considered far too much trouble for would-be epicures. We are told to use costly ingredients, often for the simple reason that they are expensive and the implication is that because they are higher-priced they must be better. But such answers to "What's for dinner?" are as rare in the South as a lack of fresh ingredients and hospitality.

A well-known writer recalling his boyhood once described the family kitchen as "a kind of holy place" where all the kids had their own tasks to perform while their mother "ministered lavishly to her family via stove and sink and cupboards and flour bin." He said that "Good cooking was a way of life and enjoyment. You did not save time, but spent it recklessly, proudly and with full reward inside those spotless four walls." It is a perfect definition of Southern cooking, which itself comes closer to defining 19th-century America than any institution we have left.

Above: a once-comfortable home illustrates the all-too-devastating effect the Civil War had on the South.

After-dinner conversation on almost any porch or freshly-swept front yard in every small town of the American South will almost inevitably come around to remembering the old days. And a comment that is sure to creep in is the observation that "We didn't know we were poor back in those days." Hard times weren't much fun – it is the good times there that are not forgotten, way down South in Dixie – but they are the heart and soul of every great cuisine, including the ones would-be gourmets celebrate, not the least of them the traditional cookery of the American South. It is the triumph of a people who made do with and thrived amidst limited resources and political unrest.

Although we enjoy the foods of other countries, anything less than real American cooking, which has assimilated the ideas of other cultures but adapted them to local produce, is never quite authentic. And the last surving authentic American cuisine may well be represented in Southern tradition. The best part is that the ingredients are relatively inexpensive, locally available, and easily combined without any complicated techniques. And remember, the people who perfected the style did it over wood-burning stoves or in front of open fireplaces. With modern kitchens, what they made look easy has never been easier.

CHAPTER ONE

Soups

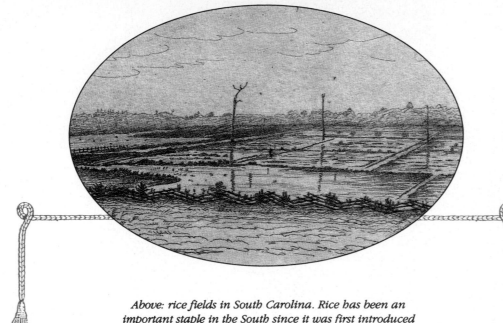

*Above: rice fields in South Carolina. Rice has been an
important staple in the South since it was first introduced
into the region by Thomas Jefferson.*

Severe poverty has characterized much of the history
of the South, particularly following the Civil War,
when cooks were forced through necessity to make the
most of what was locally abundant, using their skill to
create delicious and nutritious, though essentially
frugal, dishes. Scarcity meant that soups were often the
main meal of the day, replacing meat or fish. This has
left the South with a tradition of wholesome soups,
made with easily-available ingredients such as
peanuts and crawfish, that were substantial and
nutritious enough to be a meal in themselves.

Collard Green Soup

Georgia Peanut Soup

2 Tbsps butter
1 stalk celery, finely chopped
1 medium onion, finely chopped
1 Tbsp flour
4 cups chicken stock
½ cup chunky peanut butter
1½ cups half and half or milk
Salt and pepper to taste

GARNISH
¼ cup chopped peanuts
Paprika

In a large saucepan, melt the butter over a low heat. Add the celery and onion and sauté until they are softened, but not brown. Stir in the flour to make a smooth paste and

Among the South's numerous varieties of greens, collard greens are ubiquitous, especially at New Year's celebrations, when their color is seen as symbolizing money and good luck.

2 ham hocks
2 quarts water
1 cup Great Northern Beans, soaked overnight and drained
1 pound Chorizo sausage, sliced
1 pound white bacon, diced
1 large onion, chopped
1 clove garlic, minced
12 oz frozen, chopped collard greens
Salt and pepper to taste

Boil the ham hocks in the water for 1 hour. Add the soaked beans to the soup and simmer until tender – about 2 hours. Meanwhile, sauté the sausage, drain and set aside. Clean the frying pan, then sauté the bacon until crisp. Remove and set aside, then fry the garlic and onion in the bacon drippings. When the beans are nearly cooked, add the sautéed bacon, sausage, onion, and garlic to the pot. Cook the collard greens in a small amount of boiling water for 15 minutes, or follow the directions on the package. Add to the soup and season to taste with salt and pepper. Simmer for 45 minutes to allow the flavors to blend. Serves 10.

cook for 2-3 minutes. Gradually add the chicken stock, stirring to make a smooth sauce. Bring the soup to a boil. Blend in the peanut butter and simmer for about 15 minutes, stirring occasionally. Add the half and half to the pan and heat the soup just to boiling point. Taste and add salt and pepper if necessary. To serve, garnish each bowl of soup with chopped peanuts and a sprinkling of paprika. Serves 4-6.

The development of peanut soup is attributed to George Washington Carver an agricultural researcher who helped popularize peanuts as a major crop.

Southern-Style Potato Soup

Bisque of Garden Peas

When those peas start coming in from the garden, this is a delicious way to add variety to your menu.

3 cups peas, fresh or frozen
2 cups water
¼ cup onions, chopped
3 Tbsps butter
3 Tbsps all-purpose flour
3 cups milk or half and half
Salt and cayenne pepper to taste

Cook the fresh peas in the water, with a pinch of salt, until tender. If using frozen peas, follow the directions on the package. Cool slightly then combine the peas, water, and onions, and purée. Melt the butter in a large saucepan and stir in the flour until smooth and bubbly. Remove from the heat and stir in the milk slowly. Return to low heat and cook, stirring constantly, until the sauce thickens. Add the puréed pea mixture and stir until well blended. Season to taste with cayenne pepper and salt. Chill and serve garnished with fresh mint leaves. Serves 4.

Good potato recipes can be found wherever there is a history of hardship, and although white potatoes were a relatively late arrival for the early settlers, they sustained many families through difficult times.

1½ cups green onions, white part only, diced
½ cup onions, chopped
1 Tbsp butter
3 cups baking potatoes, peeled and diced
3 cups hot water
3 tsps salt
1 cup hot milk
½ tsp white pepper
1 cup light cream
1 cup heavy cream
¼ cup chopped chives

In a heavy 4-quart pot, melt the butter and sauté the onion until soft, but not brown. Add the potatoes, hot water and 2 tsps of the salt. Simmer, uncovered, for 30-40 minutes, or until the potatoes are soft. Liquidize the potatoes and onions, and return to the pot. Add the hot milk, and slowly bring the soup to a boil, stirring often to keep the potatoes from settling. Add the remaining salt and pepper. Remove from the heat and strain through a sieve. Cool the soup, stir, then strain again and add the light and heavy cream. Serve chilled and garnished with the chopped chives. Makes 1½ quarts.

Above left: The Governor's Palace in Colonial Williamsburg. The original palace was completed in 1720, but tragedy struck in 1781 when it was destroyed by fire. The present palace is the most elegant building in Williamsburg and is surrounded by ten acres of beautiful gardens.

She-Crab Soup

This wonderful soup from the Georgia-Carolina coastline gets its distinctive flavor from the crab eggs. If you are unable to obtain female crabs, crumble the yolk of hard-boiled eggs into the bottom of the soup plates before serving.

1 Tbsp butter
1 tsp flour
1 quart milk
2 cups white crab meat and crab eggs
½ tsp Worcestershire sauce
⅛ tsp mace
Few drops onion juice
½ tsp salt
⅛ tsp pepper

TO SERVE
4 Tbsps dry sherry, warmed
¼ pint cream, whipped
Paprika or finely chopped parsley

In the top of a large double boiler, melt the butter and blend in the flour until smooth. Add the milk gradually, stirring constantly. Add the crab meat and eggs and all of the seasonings. Cook the soup slowly for 20 minutes over hot water. To serve, place one tablespoon of warmed sherry into individual soup bowls. Add the soup and top with whipped cream. Sprinkle with paprika or finely chopped parsley. Serves 4-6.

Tomato Celery Soup

1 small onion, chopped
½ cup finely chopped celery
2 Tbsps butter
1 × 10½ oz can of tomato soup
1 can water
1 tsp chopped parsley
1 Tbsp lemon juice
1 tsp sugar
¼ tsp salt
⅛ tsp pepper

GARNISH
¼ cup unsweetened cream, whipped
Chopped parsley

Sauté the onion and celery in the butter, but do not brown. Add the tomato soup, water, parsley, lemon juice, sugar, salt, and pepper. Simmer for 5 minutes. The celery will remain crisp. To serve, pour into 4 bowls and top each with a spoonful of unsweetened whipped cream and a sprinkling of chopped parsley. Serves 4.

This soup is a short cut recipe as it uses canned tomato soup. The addition of fresh vegetables, however, makes it taste homemade.

CHAPTER TWO

Meat, Fish and Fowl

Above: the lush blue-green meadowlands of Kentucky are perfect for farming and, of course, raising horses.

Hog meat, chicken, shellfish – particularly oysters, crawfish, and clams – and fish are at the heart of traditional Southern cookery, and feature in many of the best-loved Southern dishes, from the Cajun and Creole specialties of Louisiana to soul food, and country cooking. Yet, Southern cooks through the centuries have utilized many diverse sources of meat, in particular game. For colonial settlers, and in fact right up until the Civil War, game was an important part of the average diet, with venison, squirrel, coon, opossum and duck being eaten regularly. A legacy of this past lives on, with many of these meats still making an occasional appearance on the menu.

Stuffed Soft-Shell Crab Imperial

Shrimp Creole

The spicy sauce in this recipe is used with all sorts of meats in the South, but it tastes best with shrimp.

4 Tbsps oil
1 large green pepper, seeded and cut into 1-inch pieces
2 stalks celery, sliced
2 medium onions, diced
2 cloves garlic, crushed
2 × 14 oz cans tomatoes
2 bay leaves
1 tsp cayenne pepper or Tabasco sauce
Pinch salt and pepper
Pinch thyme
2 Tbsps cornstarch mixed with 3 Tbsps dry white wine
1½ pounds shrimp, uncooked
2 cups cooked rice

Place the oil in a large saucepan and add the vegetables. Cook for a few minutes over gentle heat and add the garlic. Add the tomatoes and their juice, breaking up the tomatoes with a fork or a potato masher. Add the bay leaves, cayenne pepper or Tabasco, seasoning, and thyme, and bring to a boil. Allow to simmer for about 5 minutes, uncovered. Mix a few spoonfuls of the hot tomato liquid

Southerners have a particular love of seafood and simple, delicious recipes such as stuffed crab have remained at the heart of Southern seafood specialties.

6 soft-shell crabs

CRAB IMPERIAL MIXTURE
1 pound backfin crab meat
1 egg
⅓ cup mayonnaise
¼ cup onion, finely diced
⅓ tsp Worcestershire sauce
1 tsp dry mustard
Pinch cayenne pepper

GARNISH
Parsley sprigs
Lemon wedges

To prepare the Crab Imperial mixture first remove the crab meat from the shell carefully to keep the meat in lump form. Set aside. In a separate bowl, beat the egg and combine with the mayonnaise. Set aside a quarter of this mixture to use as a topping. Add the remaining ingredients and toss with the crab meat.
Clean the soft-shell crabs by removing the gills and viscera. Fold back the top portion of the crabs and stuff with the Imperial mixture. Bake at 350° F for 10-12 minutes. Top with the reserved mayonnaise mixture and brown under the broiler. Garnish each with a sprig of parsley and a lemon wedge. Serve hot. Serves 6.

with the cornstarch mixture and then return it to the saucepan. Bring to a boil, stirring constantly until thickened. Add the shrimp and cover the pan. Simmer over gentle heat for about 20 minutes, or until the shrimp curl and look pink and opaque. Remove the bay leaves before serving, and spoon the mixture over hot rice. Serves 4.

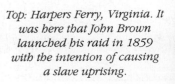

Top: Harpers Ferry, Virginia. It was here that John Brown launched his raid in 1859 with the intention of causing a slave uprising.

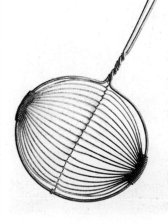

Trout Almondine

Use the freshest trout you can find to make this simple, yet elegant dish.

2 cups flour
1 tsp salt
Pinch cayenne pepper
2-3 trout, cleaned and scaled
3 oz butter
Pinch of dill
Pinch of thyme
¼ cup lemon juice
2 tbsps white wine
2 oz sliced almonds

Season the flour with salt and cayenne. Roll the trout in the flour to coat. Melt the butter in a frying pan along with the dill and thyme. Sauté the trout in the butter for approximately 3 minutes, turn and continue cooking until the fish is done – about 3-4 minutes longer. When the trout is fully cooked add the lemon juice, white wine, and almonds. Bring the liquid to a boil and simmer briefly. To serve, arrange the trout on a platter and pour the sauce on top. *Serves 2-3*

Catfish Hors D'Oeuvre

Catfish is a Southern specialty with many restaurants featuring it on their menus. It is an also an important cash crop for farmers in the South.

1 cup yellow cornmeal
½ tsp garlic salt
½ tsp cayenne
4 catfish fillets, diced
Oil for frying

Combine the cornmeal, garlic salt, and cayenne pepper. Roll the diced catfish in this mixture to coat. Fry in oil which has been heated to 375° F, or until a 1-inch cube of bread browns in 1 minute. The fish pieces will sink to the bottom of the pan. When they rise to the surface they are done. The pieces should be golden brown. Drain on paper towels and serve hot. *Serves 4-8.*

Crawfish Etouffee

*Although fresh crawfish are difficult to find outside
Louisiana, frozen crawfish or lobster meat can be used.*

6 Tbsps salted butter
¼ cup flour
1 large onion, chopped
½ cup chopped green pepper
½ cup chopped celery
1 Tbsp garlic, finely minced
30 crawfish tails
1 tsp salt
¼ tsp freshly ground black pepper
¼ tsp cayenne
1 tsp fresh lemon juice
⅓ cup thinly sliced green shallot or scallion tops
1 Tbsp finely minced fresh parsley
1 cup cold water
2 cups hot water

Melt the butter over a low heat in a heavy 5-6 quart
kettle. Gradually add the flour, and cook over a low heat
until a medium brown roux is formed. Stir in the
chopped vegetables. Continue to cook, stirring frequently,
until the vegetables are glazed and tender– about 20
minutes. Add the crawfish tails, salt, pepper, cayenne,
lemon juice, shallot tops, and parsley, and mix well.
Pour in the cold water and bring to the boil. Lower the
heat and simmer for 12 minutes, until the crawfish tails
are just tender, stirring frequently. Before serving, stir in
up to 2 cups of hot water to provide extra gravy.
The etouffee may be served in patty shells as a first course
or you can serve it over boiled rice as a main dish.
Serves 4-6.

Frog Legs

*These delicacies make a delicious
first course.*

½ cup butter
4 Tbsps olive oil
6 cloves garlic, minced
1 Tbsp cracked black peppercorns
¼ cup scallions, chopped
8 frog legs, approximately 4-inches
long
2 Tbsps white wine
1 Tbsp chopped pimentoes
¼ cup parsley, chopped
1 tsp salt
½ tsp cayenne pepper
GARNISH
4 lemon slices
4 sprigs parsley

*Melt the butter in a heavy-bottomed
sauté pan over a medium-high
heat. Add the olive oil, garlic,*

*peppercorns, and scallions. Sauté
for 1 minute, stirring constantly to
prevent the garlic from browning.
Add the frog legs and continue to
stir and cook until they are opaque
in appearance and tender to the
touch – approximately 3 minutes.
Deglaze with the white wine, then
add the pimentoes, parsley, salt,
and cayenne pepper. Serve the frog
legs with the sauce from the pan,
garnished with lemon slices and
parsley sprigs. Serves 4.*

River Road Seafood Gumbo

Recipes for gumbo abound, but as for many Cajun and Creole specialties the secret is to try one and adapt it to your own taste.

2 pounds shrimp, peeled and deveined (reserve shells to make shellfish stock)
1½ cups oil
2 cups flour
2 cups chopped onions
1 cup chopped celery
¾ cup chopped bell pepper
¼ cup chopped garlic
2 cups scallions, sliced
1 pound smoked sausage, diced
1 pound claw crab meat
1 gallon shellfish stock
2 dozen oysters, shelled
Liquor from the oysters
¼ cup parsley, chopped
¼ Tbsp filé powder
Salt and cayenne pepper to taste

To make the shellfish stock, follow the recipe for Fish Stock on page 34, substituting the shrimp shells for the fish bones. Reserve. Add the oil to a heavy-bottomed stock pot and heat over low heat. When the oil is hot, add the flour and stir constantly until a light brown roux is achieved. Add the onions, sauté for 2 minutes then add the celery, bell pepper, garlic, and the white part of the scallions. Cook for 2 minutes, stirring constantly. Add the sausage and blend well into the roux. Stir in the crab meat and 1 pound of the shrimp. Blend well into the roux until the shrimp begin to turn pink. Add the stock, 1 ladle at a time, blending after each addition until it is well incorporated. Continue adding stock until the gumbo achieves a soup-like texture. Simmer for 35 minutes, adding remaining stock to retain the volume. Add half of the scallion tops, the oyster liquor, remaining shrimp, and parsley. Cook for 5 minutes then add the oysters, remaining scallions, and filé powder. Remove the gumbo from the heat, and allow to stand for 15 minutes. Season to taste with salt and cayenne pepper. Serves 10.

Oysters Casino

Oysters were once so plentiful that they played an important part in the staple diet of the poor.

12 oysters
½ small green pepper, diced
½ small onion, diced
1 pinch seafood seasoning per oyster
2 drops lemon juice per oyster
½ cup Monterey Jack cheese, grated
3 strips bacon, cut into 1-inch pieces
TO SERVE
Butter
Lemon wedges

Clean the oysters and loosen from the shells at the muscle. Place a small amount of finely diced green pepper and onion on top of each and sprinkle with the seafood seasoning and lemon juice. Cover each oyster with grated Monterey Jack cheese and top with a piece of bacon. Bake at 350° F for 6-8 minutes. Serve with butter and lemon wedges. Serves 3-4.

Florida Seafood Stew

Florida is justifiably famous for its seafood and this stew makes excellent use of the wide variety of seafood available. In keeping with many Southern recipes the type of fish and shellfish used can be varied, so use the types which are freshest in your area.

FISH STOCK
1 quart cold water
2 pounds fish bones and fish heads
2 onions, coarsely chopped
2 sprigs parsley, chopped
3-4 celery tops, coarsley chopped
Juice of ½ lemon
Salt and freshly ground pepper to taste

STEW
⅓ cup olive oil
1 Tbsp butter
1 Tbsp fresh garlic, minced
4 Tbsps onion, chopped
1 Tbsp fresh parsley, chopped
2 tomatoes, peeled, seeded and chopped
1 Tbsp tomato paste
Pinch thyme, saffron and oregano
Salt and freshly ground pepper to taste
2-3 pounds fresh fish, boned and cut into chunks
2-3 pounds shellfish, such as lobster, shrimp, crab, clams or scallops, cleaned, but left in their shells
⅓ cup cognac or brandy
1½ cups dry white wine

First prepare the fish stock by combining the fish bones and heads with the water in a large stock pot. Bring to the boil and add the remaining ingredients. Simmer for 1 hour, skimming as necessary. Strain and set aside. To prepare the stew, heat the olive oil and butter in a large frying pan. Add the garlic, onions, parsley, tomatoes, tomato paste, and seasonings. Sauté for 3-4 minutes, then add the fish and shellfish. Stir and cook for another 1-2 minutes. Pour the cognac over the seafood. Ignite and allow to flame briefly. Transfer the stew to a stew pot, and add the white wine and the fish stock. Simmer for ten minutes before serving. Discard any shellfish whose shells have not opened. Serves 8-10.

Shrimp Remoulade

Try this recipe with sliced scallops, mussels, or clams for a variation.

1½ pounds raw unshelled large shrimp
3 Tbsps mild mustard
2 tsps horseradish
1 Tbsp paprika
1 fresh chili pepper, seeded and finely chopped
1 clove garlic, crushed
Salt
½ cup white wine vinegar
1½ cups oil
6 green onions, sliced
2 stalks celery, thinly sliced
2 bay leaves
2 Tbsps chopped parsley
Lettuce and lemon wedges

Shell the shrimp, except for the very tail ends. If desired, the shrimp may be completely shelled. Combine the mustard, horseradish, paprika, chili pepper, garlic, and salt in a deep bowl. Mix in the vinegar thoroughly. Add the oil in a thin, steady stream while beating constantly with a small whisk. Continue to beat until the sauce is smooth and thick. Add the green onions, celery, bay leaves, and chopped parsley. Cover the bowl tightly and leave in the refrigerator for several hours, or overnight. Two hours before serving, add the shrimp to the marinade and stir to coat them well. Leave in the refrigerator until ready to serve. To serve, shred the lettuce finely and place on individual serving plates. Arrange the shrimp on top and spoon over some of the marinade to serve, discarding the bay leaves. Serves 4.

Crab Smithfield

Virginia's famous Smithfield ham makes a wonderful addition to fresh crab meat in this quickly-made first course.

1 oz butter
5 oz crab meat
1 oz Smithfield ham, cut into julienne slices
GARNISH
Parsley sprigs
Lemon wedges

Melt the butter in a sauté pan. Add the crab meat and sauté for 2 minutes. Arrange the julienned ham on top and brown under the broiler for 1 minute. Garnish with sprigs of parsley and a lemon wedge before serving. Serves 2-4.

Crispy Fried Catfish

Eating catfish is a serious business in the South, and one taste of this Southern specialty will illustrate just why so many backwoods catfish restaurants still thrive.

6 catfish
1 egg
½ cup evaporated milk
1 Tbsp salt
Dash of pepper
1 cup flour
½ cup yellow cornmeal
2 tsps paprika
Oil for frying

Clean, skin, wash, and dry the catfish before cutting them into serving-sized portions. Beat the egg into the milk and stir in the salt and pepper. In a separate bowl, combine the flour, cornmeal, and paprika. Dip the cleaned fish in the milk mixture, then roll in the seasoned flour. Heat the oil in a heavy-bottomed pan to 375°F or until a 1-inch cube of bread turns golden after 1 minute. When the oil is hot enough, add the fish and brown well on both sides. When the fish are done, lift them carefully from the pan and drain them on absorbent paper. Serve very hot. Serves 6.

Above left: the bayou provides excellent fishing for both weekend fishermen and those out to catch their evening meal. Below: a hardy stove that has survived from the 1800s.

Crab Cakes with Red Pepper and Tomato Sauce

Crab cakes are a wonderful introduction to the delights of Southern seafood cooking. The addition of peppers and herbs makes these crab cakes especially tasty.

Red Pepper and Tomato Sauce

This sauce makes a good accompaniment to seafood.

4 plum tomatoes, peeled, seeded and coarsely chopped
3 red bell peppers, roasted, peeled, seeded and coarsely chopped
1 Tbsp tomato paste
3 Tbsps lemon thyme, chopped
Salt and pepper to taste
Tabasco sauce to taste
Lemon juice to taste

GARNISH
1 ear Silver Queen corn, or other white variety, shucked and removed from the cob

Combine the tomatoes and peppers in a heavy-bottomed saucepan. Simmer over medium-low heat until they are very soft. Purée in a food processor, or pass through the fine blade of a food mill. Stir in the tomato paste and leave to cool. When cool, add the lemon thyme and season with salt and pepper, Tabasco sauce, and lemon juice to taste. Blanch the corn kernels in boiling, salted water for 15 seconds, then drain and refresh in cold water. Use to garnish the sauce. Serves 4.

1 pound crab meat, picked over for shell particles
2 Tbsps red bell pepper, finely chopped
2 Tbsps yellow bell pepper, finely chopped
2 Tbsps green bell pepper, finely chopped
2 Tbsps celery, finely chopped
1 green onion, minced
2 eggs
¼ cup dried bread crumbs
1 Tbsp fresh lemon thyme, chopped
1 Tbsps flat leaf parsley, chopped
1½ tsps coarse salt
¼ tsp fresh ground pepper
Zest of one lemon, grated
Butter

TO SERVE
Sprigs of lemon thyme
Corn kernels
Red Pepper and Tomato Sauce (see left column)

Combine all the ingredients, except for the butter, lemon thyme sprigs, and the corn kernels, in a large bowl and mix well. Form the mixture into cakes 1½ inches in diameter and ½-inch thick. Sauté in butter over medium heat for approximately one minute on each side, or until the cakes are lightly browned.
To serve, place a spoonful of Red Pepper and Tomato Sauce on each plate. Arrange several crab cakes on top and garnish with sprigs of lemon thyme and kernels of corn. Serves 4.

Above: the commissary department of the Army of the Potomac, camped at Fairfax, Virginia. The Union Army was always better supplied than the Confederate. Right: the dry goods store at Harpers Ferry, Virginia.

Chicken Croquettes

Above right: a house near Cedar Mountain, Virginia, commandeered by soldiers during the Civil War.

This is a delicious and economical way to use up leftover chicken. Try serving the croquettes with Mushroom Cream Sauce (see right column).

2 cups dry bread crumbs
1½ cups chicken broth
4 cups minced cooked chicken
1 cup mushrooms, coarsely chopped
1 tsp chopped onion
½ cup chopped celery
½ tsp salt
⅛ tsp red pepper
1 Tbsp chopped parsley
Dash lemon juice
1 cup dry bread crumbs
1 beaten egg
2 Tbsps water or milk
Oil for frying

Soak the bread crumbs in the broth. Meanwhile, mix together the chicken and mushrooms, combine with the soaked bread crumbs and the rest of the croquette ingredients, and allow to cool. Divide the mixture evenly into 24 bars or squares, no thicker than 1½-inches, and chill. To cook, dip each croquette into dry bread crumbs, then into a mixture of beaten egg and water or milk, and finally into bread crumbs again. (This is the secret of good croquettes!) Fry in oil, heated to 375° F, until golden – approximately 2-4 minutes. Serves 8-12.

Mushroom Cream Sauce

This creamy sauce is a perfect partner for chicken.

3 Tbsps butter
¼ cup flour
Salt and pepper to taste
Dash paprika
1½ cups warm milk
1½ cups canned unsweetened, condensed milk
1 cup sliced fresh mushrooms
1 Tbsp butter

Melt the butter in the top of a double boiler. Whisk in the flour, salt, pepper, and paprika until well blended and smooth. Add the milk and condensed milk slowly, stirring constantly to prevent lumps. Continue to cook and stir until the sauce is smooth and thick. Lightly brown the sliced mushrooms in 1 tablespoon of butter and stir into the sauce. Check the seasoning adding more paprika, salt and pepper to taste.

Wild Duck Breasts with Raspberries

Wild ducks have been hunted in the flatlands of the South for centuries, and their distinctive flavor ensures that roast duck will remain a popular dish in Southern kitchens.

Chicken and Dumplings

1 5-pound stewing chicken
½ cup butter
Water to cover
Salt and pepper to taste

DUMPLINGS
4 cups all-purpose flour
1½ cups ice water

GARNISH
fresh or dried parsley

Place the chicken and the butter in a large pot and pour over water to cover. Boil for 2-3 hours, or until the chicken is very tender, adding extra water if necessary. Remove the chicken and allow to cool, reserving the broth. When the chicken is cool enough to handle, remove the meat, cut into serving-size pieces and return to the broth. To prepare the dumplings, make a well in the middle of the flour. Pour in the ice water and blend with a fork or with your fingers until the dough forms a ball. Roll out thinly and cut into 2-3-inch wide strips. Bring the chicken and broth to the boil and season to taste with salt and pepper. Slowly drop the dough strips into the broth. Simmer for 2-4 minutes, or until the dumplings are tender. Ladle the chicken, dumplings and broth into bowls to serve. Serves 6-8.

4 wild duck breasts
Butter for browning
Salt and pepper to taste

RASPBERRY SAUCE
1 pint raspberries
½ cup water
½ cup sugar
1 cup orange juice
Grated zest of 1 orange

GARNISH
Fresh raspberries
Fresh mint leaves

First prepare the raspberry sauce by combining the raspberries, water, sugar, and orange juice in a saucepan. Simmer the ingredients slowly for 20-35 minutes. Strain the sauce through a fine mesh sieve, then stir in the zest. Set aside while you roast the duck breasts.
To prepare the duck, heat some butter in a frying pan and place the duck, skin side down, in the hot pan. Carefully brown the skin. Remove the breasts to a roasting pan and roast on a rack for 10 to 15 minutes. Be careful not to overcook; roast only until the meat is light pink. Towards the end of the cooking time, spoon some of the raspberry sauce over the meat.
To serve, place several spoonfuls of the sauce onto each plate. Slice the meat diagonally and arrange on top of the sauce. Garnish with fresh raspberries and sprigs of mint. Serves 4.

Above: an engraving from 187_ illustrates the wealth of the lan_ along Louisiana's Gulf coast. T_ South has always been blesse_ with numerous native foods su_ as pumpkins, squash, beans, pe_ and onions, but it was the immigrants and slaves who ga_ Southern cuisine its distinct character by introducing suc_ foods as peppers, peanuts, okr_ and sweet potatoes. Facing pag_ Chicken and Dumplings.

43

Grey's Hill Roast Turkey with Cornbread Stuffing

STUFFING
2 Tbsps butter
½ cup chopped onion
2 Tbsps chopped celery
2 Tbsps green pepper
2 cups corn bread cubes
1 cup bread cubes
1 Tbsp chopped parsley
Salt to taste
Pinch thyme
½ cup or more chicken stock or water

ROAST TURKEY
10-12 pound turkey at room temperature
2 tsps salt and 2 tsps baking soda
1 tsp pepper
2 Tbsps butter, softened
4 Tbsps butter, melted
½ cup cognac

Below: the oddly shaped roots of the mangrove trees provide a convenient habitat for fish.

First prepare the stuffing. Melt the butter and sauté the onion, celery, and pepper until tender. Stir in the remaining stuffing ingredients and moisten with chicken stock or hot water.

Preheat the oven to 450° F. Wash and dry the turkey. Rub the inside of the body and neck with salt, baking soda, and pepper. Lightly stuff the cavities with the cornbread stuffing and sew or skewer closed. Tuck the wings under and fasten the legs down. Rub the surface of the bird with the softened butter and place on a rack in a shallow baking pan, breast side up. Combine the melted butter and cognac to use as a baste. Place the turkey in the preheated oven and immediately reduce the heat to 325° F. Roast uncovered for 1 hour, basting frequently. Make a loose tent out of aluminum foil and lay on top of the bird. Continue cooking for a further 3 hours, basting from time to time. If you run out of the baste, pour some boiling water into the bottom of the roasting pan, stir up the drippings and use this liquid as a baste. Remove the foil during the last 30 minutes to allow the bird to brown.

The turkey is done when the leg joint moves freely. Remove from the oven and allow the bird to stand for 20 minutes before carving.

Southern Fried Chicken

This is one way to cook that real Southern Fried Chicken!

1 chicken, fresh
Flour for dredging
Salt and pepper to taste
Oil for frying

Cut the chicken into portions and wipe dry. Dredge in flour which has been seasoned with salt and pepper. Fry in boiling oil in a skillet until golden brown. Cook only a few pieces at a time. Serves 4.

Chicken Country Captain

Georgia is the home of this spicy dish, said to have been brought back from India by an adventurous sea-captain.

Above: an engraving from 1872 of a planter's house on the Mississippi.

3 Tbsps vegetable oil
1½ cups chopped onions
1 clove garlic, minced
¾ cup chopped green pepper
1 tsp curry powder
¼ tsp thyme
⅛ tsp cayenne pepper
2 Tbsps chopped parsley
1 × 32 oz can tomatoes, drained and chopped
4 pound frying chicken, cut into serving-size pieces
1 cup flour, seasoned with salt and pepper
Oil for frying
½ cup water
½ cup currants
32 whole roasted almonds
3 cups cooked rice

Heat the oil and sauté the onions, garlic, green pepper, and curry powder in the oil until the vegetables are tender. Add the thyme, cayenne, parsley, and tomatoes. Cover, and simmer for 1 hour over a low heat. Meanwhile, sprinkle the chicken pieces with salt and pepper and dredge in the seasoned flour. Heat the oil to 375° F, add the chicken pieces and fry until just done – about 10–15 minutes. Place the cooked chicken in a roasting pan, add the water and sprinkle with the currants. Pour the simmered vegetables over, cover tightly and bake at 325° F for 1 hour.
Garnish with the roasted almonds and serve over very hot cooked rice. Serves 6.

Baked Stuffed Yellow Squash

8 medium yellow squash
4 Tbsps butter
1 onion, finely chopped
½ cup fine bread crumbs
Salt and pepper to taste
2 egg yolks, beaten
2 Tbsps Worcestershire sauce
(optional)

Cook the unpeeled squash in boiling, salted water until they are just tender – about 15 minutes. Cut off the stem end and a ½-inch thick slice off the top of each. Carefully scoop out the flesh, leaving the shell intact. Chop the flesh, together with the top slice, and drain well. Melt the butter in a heavy skillet and sauté the onion until tender and translucent. Stir in the chopped squash and most of the bread crumbs, reserving some to sprinkle on the top. Season lightly with salt and pepper. Remove the vegetables from the heat, cool slightly, then stir in the beaten egg yolks and Worcestershire sauce. Use this mixture to stuff the squash shells. Sprinkle with the reserved bread crumbs, then bake on a greased cookie sheet at 350° F for 20-25 minutes. Serves 8.

Brunswick Stew

Originally a squirrel stew, Brunswick stew has evolved into a deliciously spicy recipe with chicken replacing the squirrel meat. In Brunswick County, Virginia, the stew is cooked in vast quantities for public gatherings, and although the exact ingredients vary from town to town, the end result is always a treat.

2½ pounds chicken pieces
1 pound beef, diced
1½ pounds pork, diced
Seasoned flour
6 Tbsps butter
1½ quarts tomatoes, chopped
1½ pounds potatoes
½ pound corn on the cob
¾ pound onions
½ pound lima beans
½ pound okra
½ pound carrots
1½ quarts water
1 pint ketchup
Salt and pepper to taste

Coat all the meat lightly with seasoned flour. Heat the butter in a large skillet and brown the meat in batches. Drain the meat, and set aside. Clean and dice the potatoes, onions, okra, and carrots, but leave the lima beans and the corn on the cob whole. Place the water in an 8-quart pot and add all of the vegetables, including the tomatoes and the meat. Bring to a boil, then simmer for 1½ hours. Mix in the ketchup, stirring constantly. Cook over a medium heat for another 45 minutes. Season to taste with salt and pepper before serving. Serves 12.

Mrs. Samuel G. Stoney's Black River Pate

This is an old French Huguenot dish which has been in the Stoney family for generations.

3 parts leftover venison
Coarse black pepper and salt to taste
1 part butter

Put the venison through the finest blade of a meat grinder twice. Work the pepper into the butter and add salt to taste. Combine the venison and seasoned butter in a Pyrex dish and pound with a wooden mallet until the pâté forms a solid mass. Smooth the top and bake at 325° F for approximately 1 hour, or until golden brown. Chill before serving.
To serve, cut into thin slices and serve with hominy or salad. The pâté will keep very well in the refrigerator.

Top: an engraving from 1872 of a typical Southern household.
Above: an early illustration of George Washington and his wife.

Cooking a Pig

If you are planning a really big celebration, you might be interested to know how to cook a pig, Georgia style.

The ideal pig is one which has been either Federal or State approved, with a dressed (gutted, without head or feet) weight of 110-130lbs. The pig should be split down the breastbone, or butterflied, but not cut in two. Trim away any excess fat in the pig's inner cavity, then liberally salt the entire cavity.

The best way to cook the pig is in a barbecue pit. An easy and inexpensive pit to build is one made of cinder blocks. The pit should be four feet long, four feet wide and three feet deep, with a hole at one end big enough for a shovel to pass through. Make a cooking rack or grill out of metal, preferably stainless steel. The pit may be covered with a piece of plywood.

About ⅓ of a cord of seasoned hardwood, such as oak, hickory, pecan or mesquite, will be needed for the fire which will produce the coals needed for the cooking. Be sure to build the fire in such a way that the coals will be easy to reach through the hole with a shovel.

Build the fire well in advance and prime the pit by heating the grill for 15 minutes. Place the pig on the grill, rib side down. Arrange the coals under the two hams and two shoulders, which are the thickest parts of the pig. It is important to keep a good heat (250–350°F) under the pig at all times, so add new hot coals approximately every 30 minutes. Be careful not to burn the underside of the meat.

The pig should be ready to turn after 10 or more hours, depending on size. After turning, the pig needs constant attention. The heat of the coals will make the back fat liquify and accumulate in the middle rib area. This must be ladled away and discarded, but be careful, the fat is very flammable. During the last three hours, baste the pig with a good barbecue sauce to keep the meat from drying out. When most of the back fat has been rendered, which will take about 5 hours, the pig should be fully cooked. The pig should be cooked enough so that the meat falls off the bone. The pig will serve about 120 people.

Above left: an illustration from 1861 of salted meat being tested and weighed for the army. The use of woodcut illustrations in journals was pioneered by Harper's New Monthly, founded in 1850. Below: an engraving of Woodlands, the home of the novelist W.G. Simms, which was later destroyed during the passage of Sherman's army.

Bourbon Ribs

Try these for one of the best barbecues you ever tasted.

4 pounds beef or pork ribs

SAUCE

1 medium onion, chopped (approximately ½ cup)
½ cup light molasses
½ cup catsup
2 Tbsps orange peel, finely shredded
⅓ cup orange juice
2 Tbsps cooking oil
1 Tbsp vinegar
1 Tbsp steak sauce
½ tsp prepared mustard
½ tsp Worcestershire sauce
¼ tsp garlic powder
¼ tsp salt
¼ tsp pepper
¼ tsp hot pepper sauce
⅛ tsp ground cloves
¼ cup bourbon

Place the ribs in a large Dutch oven or saucepan and add water to cover. Bring to boil, then reduce the heat and simmer, covered, for 40-55 minutes or until the ribs are tender. Remove from the heat and drain thoroughly. While the ribs are cooking, prepare the sauce by combining all of the sauce ingredients in a pan. Bring the mixture to the boil and simmer gently, uncovered, for 15 to 20 minutes.
When the ribs have drained thoroughly, grill the ribs over medium coals on a barbecue for about 45 minutes. Turn every 15 minutes and baste with the sauce. Extra sauce can be served with the meat. Serves 6.

Bell Pepper Baked Beans

A quick and easy way to enjoy baked beans, Mississippi style!

1 × 16 oz can baked beans
1 large bell pepper, cut into small strips
1 small onion, chopped
1 Tbsp paprika
1 Tbsp prepared mustard
3 Tbsps brown sugar
⅛ tsp powdered dried basil
⅛ tsp powdered dried oregano

Combine all the ingredients in a large baking dish. Bake, uncovered, at 350° F, for 25-35 minutes, or until the sauce is thick and the onion and pepper are tender. Serves 6.

Above left: built in 1840, Cedar Grove in Vicksburg, Mississippi, a classic example of the Greek-Revival style.

Above: Bourbon Street in New Orleans' French Quarter is the main attraction for people seeking a taste of the city's nightlife.

Lorenzo's Country Ham

Southerners have always had a particular passion for cured ham, and although Smithfield is home of the most famous hams, country hams can be found in many other rural locations.

1 whole country ham, uncooked
4 cups water
½ cup sugar
1 cup fine dry bread crumbs

Soak the ham for 12 hours. Wash thoroughly and scrub off all of the mold. Preheat the oven to 400° F. Place the ham on a large sheet of heavy duty aluminum foil and put in a roasting pan. Join the sides of the foil to form a container. Pour in the water and seal the top of the foil. Roast for 20 minutes, then turn off the oven for 3 hours, leaving the ham inside and the oven door closed. Reheat the oven to 400° F and, when it has come up to temperature, roast for another 20 minutes. Turn off the oven and leave the ham inside for 6-8 hours, or overnight. Do not open the oven door during the entire cooking cycle. When the cooking time is up, remove the ham from the foil and, while still warm, carefully remove the skin and all but a very thin layer of the fat. Sprinkle the ham with the sugar and bread crumbs and bake, uncovered, at 400° F for 15 minutes, or until the ham is browned. Cool and slice as thinly as possible to serve.

Broiled Flounder

This simple, tasty treatment of flounder has been served in the South for generations.

2 eggs, separated
Pinch salt, pepper and dry mustard
1 cup peanut oil
4 Tbsps pickle relish
1 Tbsp chopped parsley
1 Tbsp lemon juice
Dash of Tabasco
4 double fillets of flounder

Place the egg yolks in a blender, food processor or deep bowl. Blend in the salt, pepper, and mustard. Add the oil slowly in a thin, steady stream with the machine running or while beating constantly with a whisk. Mix in the relish, parsley, lemon juice, and Tabasco. Beat the egg whites until stiff but not dry and fold into the mayonnaise. Broil the fish about 2 inches from the heat source for about 6-10 minutes. Spread the sauce over each fillet and broil for 3-5 minutes longer, or until the sauce puffs and browns lightly. Serves 4.

Jambalaya

This hearty one-pot meal has been popular in New Orleans for longer than anyone can remember. Although seen as a Cajun or Creole specialty, it is essentially a dish that has always utilized whatever the cook has in the store cupboard.

1 pound pork, cut into half inch cubes
1 Tbsp garlic powder
4 cups water
1 pound boneless chicken meat
1 pound onions, chopped
1 bell pepper, chopped
1 pound smoked sausage, diced
1 can cream of mushroom soup
1 bunch scallions, chopped
¼ cup parsley, chopped
1 pound uncooked Uncle Ben's rice
10 drops Worcestershire sauce
Salt and pepper to taste

Season the pork with salt, pepper, and the garlic powder a few hours before you plan to cook. Pour ½ cup of the water into a 6 quart pot and add the seasoned pork. Cook over medium heat for 30 minutes. Add the chicken and cook for a further 10 minutes. Stir in the onions and bell pepper and continue cooking for 15 minutes, stirring often to avoid sticking. Mix in the smoked sausage and simmer for an additional 10 minutes. Next add the cream of mushroom soup, the rest of the water, the scallions, parsley, and rice. Bring to a boil and add the Worcestershire sauce, salt, and pepper. Cover and cook over a low heat for 30 minutes, stirring once after 15 minutes. Serves 10.

Peppered Ham

This ham makes a good table center piece when entertaining.

1 fully cooked or cured ham
Liquid Smoke
Sorghum molasses
Coarse ground pepper

Trim the excess fat off the ham and rub it with Liquid Smoke and sorghum molasses. Sprinkle generously with coarse ground pepper to cover. Wrap the ham in aluminum foil, and refrigerate overnight. The next day, remove the foil and place the ham in a shallow roasting pan. Bake at 325° F for 3½ to 4 hours. Serves 8-10.

Above left: an Acadian homestead in Louisiana in 1867. Facing page: New Orleans' fashionable Vieux Carré is best viewed at a leisurely pace from a brightly colored, horse-drawn carriage. Below: an intriguing view of the French Quarter is provided by this etching from the 19th century.

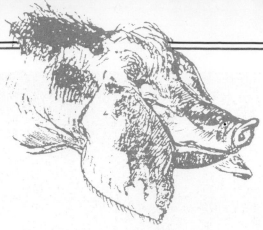

Marinaded Pork Loin with Orange Sauce

Orange adds a refreshing tang to succulent pork.

5 pound loin of pork or
8 pork chops, 1-inch thick

MARINADE
½ cup lemon juice
½ cup soy sauce
½ cup red wine
½ tsp pressed garlic
2 tsps ground ginger

ORANGE SAUCE
⅔ cup sugar
½ tsp cinnamon
20 whole cloves, tied in a cheesecloth bag
1 Tbsp grated orange rind
1 cup orange juice
1 Tbsp cornstarch
½ tsp salt
8 orange slices, cut into halves

Combine the marinade ingredients and pour over the pork. Cover and refrigerate overnight, turning occasionally. Remove the meat, reserving the marinade for basting. Roast at 350° F, basting often with the reserved marinade, for approximately 2½ hours, or fry the pork chops until they are browned. To prepare the orange sauce, combine the sugar, spices, orange rind, orange juice, cornstarch, and salt in a saucepan and cook over a medium heat, stirring frequently, until the sauce is thickened and clear. Remove the bag of cloves and add the orange slices. To serve, arrange the meat on a serving platter and pour the orange sauce over the meat. Serves 8.

Above: the peaceful beauty of Magnolia Gardens, a wonderland of trees and flowering shrubs situated north of Charleston.

Roast Leg of Lamb

Serve with baked yams and baked Vidalia onions.

1 × 5-6 pound leg of lamb
Salt and pepper to taste
6 cloves garlic, crushed
3-4 Tbsps dried rosemary
Several sprigs fresh rosemary

Preheat the oven to 450° F. Rub the lamb with salt, pepper, crushed garlic, and dried rosemary. Place the meat in a roasting pan and lay sprigs of fresh rosemary on top. Brown the lamb in the hot oven for approximately 15 minutes, or until the meat is sealed, then lower the temperature to 350° F and roast for about 10 minutes per pound (roughly 1¼-1½ hours total). The rosemary and garlic enhance the delicious flavor of the lamb. The cooking time suggested will produce a medium-rare roast. If you prefer your meat a bit more done, increase the cooking time slightly. Serves 6-8.

Pan-Fried Pork Chops

Pork chops are given a delightful Southern flavor with addition of cornmeal and pepper.

4 × 8 oz center cut pork loin chops
½ cup all-purpose flour
¼ cup stone-ground cornmeal
½ tsp salt
¼ tsp black pepper, ground
⅛ tsp cayenne pepper
⅛ tsp paprika
Peanut oil for cooking

Combine the flour, cornmeal, salt, and spices, and dredge the pork chops in this seasoned mixture until they are coated. Heat a cast-iron or other heavy-bottomed frying pan over a medium high heat for 3 minutes, then brush the pan with a thin film of peanut oil. When the oil just smokes, add the coated pork chops and reduce the heat to medium. Cook for 4 minutes, then turn the chops. Cover the pan and cook for a further 4 to 5 minutes, or until the meat is juicy, but no longer pink at the bone.
Serves 6.

Top: the Raleigh Tavern at Colonial Williamsburg was once a local political and social center where figures such as Washington, Jefferson, and Harvey gathered.

Parke's Salamagundi

This attractive salad is an early summer favorite in Virgina.

1 pound Virginia ham, julienned
1 pound chicken or turkey, julienned
6 hard-cooked eggs, sliced
8 oz anchovy fillets
4 oz sardines in olive oil
Celery hearts
Assorted salad greens
Assorted pickles
1 cup or more of your favorite French dressing

Arrange the meat, eggs, and fish in a circular pattern on a large serving platter. Surround with the celery hearts, salad greens, and pickles. Pour a light coating of French dressing over all just before serving. Serves 6-8.

CHAPTER THREE

Side Dishes

Above: City Point, Virginia, was General Grant's headquarters and supply base during the Civil War.

Preparing and cooking the wide variety of vegetables that grow in the South has become something of an art form. Salt, sugar, cream, butter, and chunks of salt pork or bacon are among the ingredients that are traditionally used to accompany vegetables, providing them with a unique and hearty flavor. Though the use of such rich ingredients is at odds with the current trend towards healthy eating, reducing the quantities of such ingredients makes the end result less unhealthy, yet still retains the character that is one of the hallmarks of Southern cookery.

Old-Fashioned Cole Slaw

This delicious cole slaw is perfect for an outdoor party or picnic. You can scale down the recipe for smaller groups.
The origins of cole slaw are thought to be Dutch, but the dish has become a particular Southern favorite served with fried catfish and Hush Puppies.

2 medium heads cabbage, finely shredded
2 large carrots, finely shredded
DRESSING
2 cups mayonnaise
1 tsp sugar
½ tsp dried mustard
½ tsp pepper
⅓ cup vinegar or lemon juice
1 tsp salt

Toss the cabbage and carrots together to make up the salad. Combine the dressing ingredients and blend well. Pour the dressing over the vegetables and mix well. Chill the cole slaw before serving. Serves 12.

Butter Bean Salad

The South is blessed with numerous varieties of beans. A cheap and plentiful source of nourishment, they have remained a much-loved side-dish for generations.

30 oz fresh or frozen butter beans
4 cups water
1 tsp salt
4 hard-cooked eggs, chopped
1 small onion, finely grated
1 cup mayonnaise
¾ tsp prepared mustard
¾ tsp Worcestershire sauce
¾ tsp hot pepper sauce

Boil the butter beans in the water and salt for 40 minutes. Drain, then combine with the rest of the ingredients. Refrigerate the salad overnight and serve on a bed of lettuce. Serves 8.

Above left: a restored cottage near Hodgenville, Kentucky, illustrates the basic furnishings and utensils of a household in 1815.

Baked Yams

The addition of Bourbon, cream and nutmeg make these yams really tasty.

6 yams
2 Tbsps butter
3 tsps brown sugar
2 tsps Bourbon whiskey
¼ cup cream, warmed
½ tsp salt
Pinch nutmeg
¼ cup raisins
¼ cup toasted pecans

Scrub the yams and bake at 400° F for approximately 50 minutes, or until soft. While still hot, scoop out the pulp and mash well. Add the remaining ingredients, except for the raisins and pecans and whip until fluffy. Fold in the raisins and pecans just before serving. Serves 4.

Curried Okra

Okra was brought to the South from Africa with the slave trade and was quickly absorbed into the cuisine, most notably in New Orleans. Although the basis for one of South's most famous recipes – Gumbo – it is just as delicious coated in cornmeal and pepper, and fried.

1 pound okra
1½ cups cornmeal
1 tsp salt
¼ tsp cayenne pepper
Oil for frying

Wash the okra, but do not dry. Trim the okra and cut into thick slices. Combine the cornmeal and the seasonings. Roll the okra in the cornmeal until well coated. Fry in hot oil in a skillet until golden brown. Drain the okra on paper towels before serving. Serves 4-6.

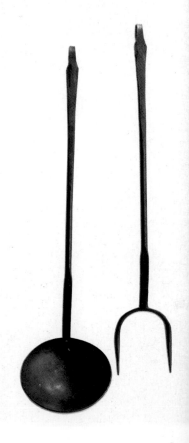

Turnip Greens

Of the many different varieties of greens popular in the South, turnip greens are the most common. The practice of boiling vegetables with meat is an age-old tradition that has stood the test of time.

2 oz lean salt pork
2 cups boiling water
2 pounds turnip greens
Salt to taste

Rinse the salt pork, score several times and add to the boiling water. Simmer rapidly for 15 minutes. Meanwhile, wash the greens thoroughly and remove any tough stems. Tear into small pieces. Add to the pork, packing into the saucepan if necessary. Cover and simmer over medium heat for 30 minutes, or until the greens are tender. Taste the broth halfway through the cooking time and add salt if necessary. Serves 4.

Facing page: Turnip Greens. Above right: the fertile plains of Georgia. Above: an etching depicting a scene from a plantation near New Orleans. Below: the state seal of Louisiana.

LOUISIANA.

Sweet Potato Souffle

Sweet potato dishes come very swee in the Southern states.

1½ pounds sweet potatoes, washed but not peeled
1 egg
1 oz margarine
1¼ cups sugar
1 Tbsp evaporated milk
2 tsps vanilla

TOPPING
¾ cup light brown sugar
1½ oz margarine, melted
¼ cup pecans

Boil the sweet potatoes until they are soft. Peel them while they are still hot, and place them in the larg bowl of an electric mixer. Mix at low speed and add the remaining ingredients, except the topping ingredients. Place this mixture in large baking dish. Combine all of the topping ingredients thoroughl; spread over the potatoes and bake at 375° F for approximately 15-20 minutes, or until set. Serves 4-6

Hush Puppies

Baked Vidalia Onions

Vidalia onions are large, sweet onions which are flat at both ends. They are grown in the area surrounding Vidalia, Georgia, and are delicious both cooked and raw.

To prepare, peel off the outer skin of the onion and cut a thin slice off both ends so that the onion will sit flat. Cut a small well into one end. Place a bouillon cube inside and cover with a pat of butter. Wrap the onion with a square of heavy aluminum foil. Place the wrapped onions on a baking sheet and bake at 350° F for 1½-2 hours, or until the onion is soft. Loosen the foil and transfer the onion to a small bowl using a slotted spoon. Pour the juices from the cooked onion and butter over the onion to serve.

The essential accompaniment to fried fish, Hush Puppies have become a national favorite. Argument still rages over the origins of the recipe, but whoever invented the dish it tastes wonderful, "authentic" or not!

1 egg, well beaten
⅔ cup milk
1½ cups white cornmeal
½ cup flour, sifted
½ tsp sugar
1 tsp baking powder
½ tsp salt
1 bunch (approximately 1 cup) fresh green onions, finely chopped
Pinch red pepper
Pinch garlic powder
Oil for frying

Mix together the egg, milk, cornmeal, flour, sugar, baking powder, and salt until well blended and smooth. Add the green onions, red pepper, and garlic powder. Shape the dough into small balls. If the dough is too soft, add more cornmeal. Heat the oil to 360° F, add the Hush Puppies and fry until they are browned. Drain on absorbent paper. Makes about 24.

Facing page: Culpepper Court House, Virginia, captured by the Confederates in August 1862.

CHAPTER FOUR

Breads and Biscuits

Above: a wood engraving from 1882 of Montpelier, the home of President Madison. Right: a baker using a period range in the working museum at Colonial Williamsburg.

For early colonists the recipes for simple cornbreads given to them by the indigenous Indians were vital for survival, and in many cases literally meant the difference between life and death. These breads have remained an important part of cookery in the South and variations of the original recipes still survive. Today, the number and variety of breads and biscuits baked in the homes of the South is vast. Specialties like beignets, Sally Lunn buns, beaten biscuits, and buttermilk biscuits are among the most popular recipes and are perfect examples of the diverse influences that have come into play to create what we think of as Southern cooking.

Beignets

A night on the town in New Orleans is not complete without stopping for chicory coffee and fresh hot beignets.

2 tsps dried yeast or 1/3 oz fresh yeast
1/2 cup milk, warmed to blood temperature
1/8 cup sugar
1/2 tsp salt
1 egg, beaten
1¾ cups bread flour
1/8 cup butter, softened
Oil for frying
Confectioners' sugar

Dissolve the yeast in the warm milk, then add the sugar, salt, and beaten egg. Gradually add half of the flour, stirring until well blended, then mix in the softened butter. Gradually add the rest of the flour until the dough is very stiff and can only be mixed with your hands. Place the dough in a warm bowl and cover with a towel. Leave it to rise in a warm place for approximately 1 hour, or until it has doubled in bulk. Knead gently on a floured surface, then roll out to a 1/4-inch thickness. Cut the dough into rectangles approximately 2½ × 3½ inches and place on a lightly floured pan. Cover with a towel and leave to rise for approximately 35 minutes. Deep fry in oil which has been heated to 360° F, turning once when the bottom side has browned. Drain on paper towels, then dust generously with confectioners' sugar. Makes 20.

Above right: Angel Biscuits. Facing page: Beignets. Above: the Confederate treasury issued its own notes during the Civil War, but the currency diminished rapidly in value as the war progressed.

Angel Biscuits

Angel biscuits are like their name—heavenly!

5 cups all-purpose flour
1 tsp baking powder
1 tsp salt
¾ cup vegetable shortening
1 package yeast (about 1 oz)
1/2 cup warm water
2 Tbsps sugar
2 cups milk

Sift together the flour, baking powder, and salt and cut in the shortening with a pastry cutter until the mixture resembles coarse bread crumbs. Dissolve the yeast in the warm water and stir in the sugar. Add the yeast mixture along with the milk to the dry ingredients and stir until the mixture is moist. To make biscuits, roll the dough onto a floured surface to a 1/2-inch thickness. Cut with a biscuit cutter and bake on greased cookie sheets, baking at 400° F for 10-12 minutes, or until the biscuits are lightly browned. Makes approximately 50 biscuits.

Blueberry Breakfast Muffins

Special Yeast Rolls

These tasty light yeast rolls are a great favorite with visitors to the South.

1 cup hot water
1 tsp salt
6 Tbsps shortening
⅓ cup sugar
1 egg, at room temperature, lightly beaten
1½ packages (1½ Tbsps) dried yeast, dissolved in 3 Tbsps lukewarm water
3½-4½ cups flour, sifted twice

Combine the hot water, salt, shortening, and sugar in a large bowl and mix thoroughly using a wooden spoon. Allow to cool to lukewarm, then add the egg, yeast, and half of the flour. Mix well and add enough flour so that the mixture is no longer sticky, using more flour than specified if necessary. Knead the dough 4 or 5

Fresh or frozen blackberries can be used instead of blueberries if you wish. Muffins like this make it worth getting up on a cold morning!

1 egg
½ cup milk
¼ cup vegetable oil
½ cup sugar
1½ cups flour
2 Tbsps baking powder
½ tsp salt
1 cup blueberries, fresh or frozen

Beat the egg with a fork and stir in the milk and the oil. Combine the dry ingredients and add to the egg mixture, blending just until the flour is moistened. The batter will be lumpy. Carefully stir in the blueberries. Bake in greased muffin tins for 20-25 minutes at 400° F, or until a toothpick inserted in the center of a muffin comes out clean. Makes 12.

Above left: one of the reconstructed log cabins at Charles Towne Landing, an exhibition park on the site of the first permanent settlement in South Carolina. Facing page: a display of traditional baking skills at Colonial Williamsburg.

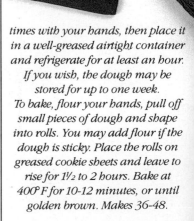

times with your hands, then place it in a well-greased airtight container and refrigerate for at least an hour. If you wish, the dough may be stored for up to one week.
To bake, flour your hands, pull off small pieces of dough and shape into rolls. You may add flour if the dough is sticky. Place the rolls on greased cookie sheets and leave to rise for 1½ to 2 hours. Bake at 400° F for 10-12 minutes, or until golden brown. Makes 36-48.

Corn Bread

This old Southern dish is still a great favorite.

2 cups self-rising cornmeal or
2 cups cornmeal plus 3 tsps baking powder
3 Tbsps flour
1 Tbsp sugar
¼ cup + 2 Tbsps vegetable oil
1¾ cups buttermilk
1 egg

Preheat a greased 9 × 9 inch pan at 425° F. Combine all the ingredients in a bowl and blend well. Pour the batter into the hot pan and bake for 20 minutes, until brown. Makes 9-16 squares.

Biscuits

These are the regular biscuits of the South, and this basic recipe is not much altered from the original. This recipe makes a lot of biscuits, so if you only need a regular amount, try using half or quarter quantities.

2½ pounds self-rising flour
1 pound shortening
1 quart buttermilk

Sift the flour into a bowl and blend in the shortening with a pastry cutter. When thoroughly mixed, stir in the buttermilk. Quickly knead the mixture for about ½ minute. Roll out on a lightly floured board to a thickness of ¼-½ inch, and cut with a 2-inch biscuit cutter. Bake on well greased cookie sheets at 425° F for 10-15 minutes, or until golden brown. Makes about 150.

Above: an early engraving of Mount Vernon, George Washington's beloved home on the Potomac.

CHAPTER FIVE

Desserts

*Above: an evocative recreation of an overseer's cottage at
the Rural Life Museum, Louisiana State University.
Right: Georgia Peach Pie.*

People from the South are renowned for their sweet
tooth and desserts are often regarded as the jewel
in the crown of Southern cooking, with a significant
number of pages in many a cook book being set aside
for cakes, pies, and puddings. This emphasis may in
part be explained by the fact that Southerners are
passionate about entertaining and hospitality, and
a sweet finale to a meal (no matter how basic), has
always provided the perfect answer to ensuring
your guests feel especially welcome. Of course, a
sheer love of sweet things and the long-established
baking tradition in the South, cannot be left out
of the equation.

Georgia Pecan Cake

½ cup margarine
½ cup shortening
2¼ cups sugar
5 eggs, separated
2½ cups all-purpose flour
1 tsp soda
1 cup buttermilk
2 Tbsps vanilla extract
½ cup grated coconut
2 cups pecans, chopped

ICING
½ cup margarine
1 pound cream cheese
2 pounds confectioners' sugar
3 Tbsps vanilla
¾ cup pecans, chopped

Using an electric mixer, cream together the margarine, shortening, and sugar for 15 minutes on medium speed. Add the egg yolks and continue to mix on low for 5 minutes. Sift the flour and soda together 3 times and add to the mixing bowl alternately with the buttermilk, beginning and ending with the flour. Turn off the mixer and fold in the vanilla extract, coconut, and pecans. Beat the egg whites until stiff, and gently fold in the cake batter. Grease and flour 3 × 9-inch cake pans and divide the mixture between them. Bake at 350° F for 30-35 minutes, or until the cake springs back when touched lightly in the center. Cool for 15 minutes in the pans before turning the layers out on to a rack. While the cakes are cooling, prepare the icing. Cream together all of the icing ingredients, except for the pecans. When the cakes are completely cool, spread the icing thickly on top of each cake and sprinkle ¼ cup of the chopped pecans on top. Place the cakes on top of each other to make a three layered cake. Serves 8-10.

Georgia Peach Pie

The South has many recipes for peaches, as it is the major product in the Southern states.

4 cups fresh peaches, washed, peeled and sliced
1 unbaked 9-inch pie shell, plus pastry top
3 egg yolks
3 Tbsps flour
1 cup sugar
½ cup butter, melted

Preheat the oven to 400° F. Place the prepared peaches in the pie shell. Blend the egg yolks, flour, sugar, and melted butter in a bowl. Pour this mixture evenly over the peaches. Cover with the pastry top and seal around the edges. Cut several slits to allow the steam to escape. Bake for 50 minutes, or until the pastry is golden brown. Serves 6-8.

Above left: Monticello, the beautiful home of Thomas Jefferson, is regarded as a classic example of American architecture. Above: the popular Greek Revival style is evident in the architecture of Susina Plantation, near Beachton, Georgia.

Key Lime Pie

This famous dessert from the Keys is delightfully sharp and refreshing. Unfortunately, Florida has lost many of its lime groves through successive hurricanes and it is often necessary to substitute a more common lime juice.

Shaker Lemon Pie

The Kentucky Shakers have a history of enjoying hearty, satisfying food and this dessert is one of many delicious specialties.

PASTRY
2 cups all-purpose flour
1 tsp salt
⅓ cup shortening
⅓ cup butter, chilled
5 Tbsps cold water

FILLING
2 large lemons
2 cups sugar
4 eggs, well beaten

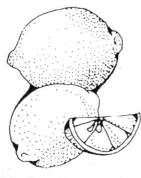

To prepare the pastry, combine the flour and salt in a bowl. Cut in the shortening and butter until the mixture resembles coarse bread crumbs. Gradually sprinkle on the cold water and blend lightly with a

CRUST
1½ cups graham cracker crumbs
½ cup sugar
½ cup butter or margarine, melted

FILLING
2 eggs
15 oz sweetened condensed milk
½ cup Key Lime juice
¼ tsp salt

TOPPING
1 cup sour cream
⅓ cup sugar
⅛ tsp salt

GARNISH
Graham cracker crumbs
Grated lime rind

First prepare the crust by blending together the crust ingredients. Press the mixture firmly into a 9-inch pie plate. Bake at 350° F for 10 minutes. To prepare the filling, beat the eggs and milk together. Add the lime juice and salt. Pour the filling into the prepared crust and bake at 350° F for 10 minutes, or until set. Meanwhile, prepare the topping by combining the sour cream, sugar, and salt. When the filling has set, spread this topping over the pie. Bake at 425° F for 5 minutes to allow the topping to set. Garnish the pie before serving. Serve cold. Serves 6-8.

Above left: Shaker Lemon Pie.
Facing page: Key Lime Pie.

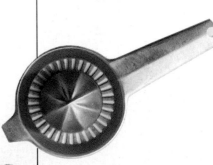

fork, until you can just gather the dough into a ball. Divide the dough into 2 pieces and leave to rest in a cool place for at least ½ hour. Roll out one of the pieces and line a 9-inch pie plate. Roll out the second piece to form a top crust.

To make the filling, wash the lemons and slice them paper thin, rind and all. Cover with the sugar and let stand for at least two hours, (overnight is better), stirring occasionally. Add the beaten eggs and mix well. Turn the filling into the lined pie dish. Cover with the top crust and cut several slits near the center. Bake at 450° F for 15 minutes, then reduce heat to 375° F and bake for about 20 minutes, or until a knife inserted near the edge of the pie comes out clean. Cool before serving. Serves 6-8.

Strawberry Shortcake

Strawberry shortcake is a sure sign of summer, certain to bring back happy memories of days spent picking and eating strawberries.

2 cups flour
3 tsps baking powder
1 Tbsp sugar
¼ tsp salt
½ cup shortening
⅔ cup milk
1 egg, beaten

TOPPING

½ cup heavy cream
½ tsp vanilla extract
1 tsp confectioners' sugar
1 quart fresh strawberries
¼ cup sugar

To mix the shortcake, sift together the dry ingredients, then cut in the shortening. Stir in the milk and egg. Knead the dough lightly and shape to fill a well greased 9-inch round baking pan. Bake at 425° F for 20 minutes. Set the cake aside to cool while you prepare the topping. To make the topping, whip the cream and fold in the vanilla extract and confectioners' sugar. Set aside 5 large, well-shaped strawberries to decorate the top of the shortcake. Crush the remaining berries with the granulated sugar.
To assemble the shortcake, cut the layer in half. Spread half of the crushed strawberries on the lower half. Top with half of the whipped cream and place the upper half of the cake on top. Decorate the top of the shortcake with the reserved strawberries. Serves 6–8.

Above: the Marquis de Lafayette, who fought with American colonists against the British. Below: Steamboat House in New Orleans.

Banana Pudding

Banana pudding in one form or another is a firmly established favorite in the South.

1 pint milk
2 bananas, sliced
½ cup sugar
3 Tbsps cornstarch
¼ tsp salt
1 tsp vanilla
1 tsp butter

Heat the milk and add the sliced bananas. Sift together the sugar, cornstarch, and salt. Stir in some of the hot milk to make a smooth paste, then stir the paste into the rest of the milk. Cook over a low heat, stirring constantly until thickened. Finally, blend in the vanilla and butter. Pour into 4 dessert glasses and chill before serving. Serves 4.

Top: Magnolia Gardens, on the outskirts of Charleston, South Carolina. Dating from the 19th century, the gardens contain a wonderful variety of azaleas, camellias, and flowering shrubs.

Big Mommy's Floating Islands

Use your imagination to vary the flavorings in this spectacular dessert.

CUSTARD
2 cups whole milk
3 egg yolks or 2 whole eggs
¼ cup sugar
⅛ tsp salt
½ tsp vanilla extract
A flavoring, such as nutmeg, amaretto, grated orange, or lemon peel

"ISLANDS"
3 egg whites
1 tsp cream of tartar
1 Tbsp sugar

To prepare the custard, scald the milk. Beat the eggs lightly, and add the sugar and salt. Add this mixture to the hot milk, stirring constantly. Cook in the top of a double boiler, stirring often, until the mixture thickens and coats the back of the spoon. Cool and flavor the mixture with the vanilla extract. Chill the custard while you prepare the "Islands". Beat the egg whites and cream of tartar until stiff, then gradually beat in the sugar to make a meringue with stiff peaks. Using a large tablespoon, float the meringues onto a roasting pan filled with hot milk or water. Brown in a preheated 400° F oven. Remove from the pan and drain.
To assemble the dessert, pour the chilled custard into a serving bowl. Using a slotted spoon, arrange the drained meringues on top. Serves 8–10.

Nelly Custis' Maids of Honor

These tarts originally came from England, but were very popular in early America.

Pastry to line 8-10 3½-inch tart pans
2 eggs
½ cup sugar
½ cup almond paste
1-2 Tbsps sherry
2 Tbsps melted butter
1 Tbsp lemon juice
2 Tbsps flour
8-10 tsps strawberry or raspberry jam

Use the pastry to line the tart pans and arrange them on a cookie sheet. Beat the eggs until very light and fluffy. Gradually beat in the sugar. Soften the almond paste with the sherry, butter, and lemon juice. Add this mixture to the beaten eggs. Drop 1 teaspoon of jam into each tart shell and fill with the batter. Bake at 350° F for about 45 minutes, or until puffed, golden, and firm. Makes 8-10 tarts.

Cherries Jubilee

This spectacular dessert is really simple to make, and delicious to eat! If you cannot buy the canned Oregon Bing cherries, buy the best canned cherries available.

1 × 17 oz can pitted fancy Oregon Bing cherries
1 Tbsp cornstarch
4 Tbsps butter
¼ cup sugar
¼ cup brandy

TO SERVE
Vanilla ice cream

In a bowl, stir ½ cup of the cherry juice from the can into the cornstarch and set aside. Melt the butter and sugar in a heavy skillet over a low heat. Add the cherries and the rest of the juice to the skillet and stir to coat, then blend in the cornstarch mixture. Cook and stir over low heat until thickened. Place the mixture in a warm chafing dish. When ready to serve, pour the brandy over the cherries and ignite. When the flames die down, serve over vanilla ice cream. Serves 4-6.

Jefferson Davis Pie

Named in honor of one of the heroes of the Confederacy, this pie is sure to please.

1 Tbsp flour
1 Tbsp cornmeal
2 cups sugar
4 eggs
¼ cup butter, melted
¼ cup lemon juice
1 Tbsp grated lemon rind
¼ cup milk
1 × 9-inch unbaked pie shell

Sift the flour and cornmeal into the sugar. Beat the eggs slightly and add to the sugar mixture, blending well. Add the butter, lemon juice, lemon rind, and milk. Pour this filling into the unbaked pie shell. Bake at 350° F for 50-60 minutes, or until the filling is set and the center is firm. Serves 8.

Lady Baltimore Cake

1 cup butter
3 cups sugar
4 eggs
3½ cups cake flour
4 tsps baking powder
1 cup milk
2 tsps vanilla extract
2 tsps almond extract
½ cup water

FROSTING

2 cups sugar
⅔ cup water
2 tsps corn syrup
2 egg whites, beaten stiffly
2 cups seedless raisins, finely chopped and soaked
overnight in sherry or brandy, if desired
2 cups pecans or walnuts, finely chopped
12 figs, finely chopped and soaked overnight in sherry or
brandy, if desired
Almond and vanilla extract, to taste

*Using an electric mixer, cream the butter. Add 2 cups of
the sugar gradually and beat to the consistency of
whipped cream. Add the eggs one at a time and beat
thoroughly. Sift together the flour and baking powder
three times. Using a wooden spoon to blend, add
alternately with the milk. Grease 2× 11-inch cake pans,
divide the batter between them, and bake at 350° F for 30
minutes, or until done. While the cakes are baking, add
the remaining cup of sugar and the water to a saucepan
and heat until the mixture thickens. Flavor with the
almond and vanilla extract and remove from the heat.
When the cake is baked, cool in the pans for 10 minutes,
then turn the layers out onto a rack for complete cooling.
As soon as you remove the layers from the pans, spread
the prepared syrup on top.*
*To prepare the frosting, combine the sugar, water, and
syrup in a saucepan. Cook until the mixture forms a firm
ball when a spoonful is dropped into cold water. Pour
this syrup gradually into the stiffly beaten egg whites,
beating constantly. Add the raisins, nuts, and figs.
Finally, stir in the almond and vanilla extracts to taste.
When the cake is cool, spread this frosting between the
layers and on the top and sides of the cake.*
Serves 8–10.

Apple Torte

*Serve this delicious dessert warm or
cold with vanilla ice cream.*

⅔ cup flour, sifted
3 tsps baking powder
½ tsp salt
1½ cups sugar
3 tsps vanilla
2 eggs, beaten
2 cups apples, peeled, cored and
diced
1 cup pecans or walnuts, chopped

*Sift together the flour, baking
powder, and salt. Set aside. In a
separate bowl, combine the sugar,
vanilla, and beaten eggs. Stir in the
dry ingredients, apples, and nuts.
Pour the batter into a buttered 8×
12× 4-inch baking dish. Bake at
350° F for 45 minutes or until a
knife inserted in the center comes
out clean. Serves 6-8.*

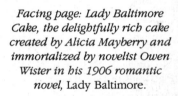

*Facing page: Lady Baltimore
Cake, the delightfully rich cake
created by Alicia Mayberry and
immortalized by novelist Owen
Wister in his 1906 romantic
novel,* Lady Baltimore.

Index

ACKNOWLEDGEMENTS

The publishers would like all those organizations and individuals who gave their time and provided recipes. Special thanks are due to the following: Art Smith and Liz Williams, The Governor's Mansion, Tallahasee; Sarahlyn Latham, The Willis House, Milledgeville, GA; Sturdivant Museum Association, Selma, AL; Elizabeth C. Kremer from the *Trustees House Daily Fare*, Pleasant Hill, Kentucky; Brice and Shirley Phillips, Phillips Waterside, Norfolk, VA; Gary Ketchum, Creative Culinary Systems, Little Rock, AR; Liza, The Governor's Mansion, Little Rock, AR; Martin Laffey, Delta Point River Restaurant, Vicksburg, MS; John D. Folse, LaFitte's Landing, Donaldsonville, LA; Chef Heinz Eberhard, Gourmet Galley, Palm Beach, FL; Ann Hall, Grey Oaks, Vicksburg, MS; Ben Barker, Fearrington House, Chapel Hill, NC; Ridgewells Caterer Inc.; Joan Smith, Editor, *Woodlawn Plantation Cookbook*, Mount Vernon, VA; Cecil L. McMillan, *The Once in a Lifetime Cookbook*, Bennett A. Brown III, Lowcountry Barbecue Catering, Atlanta, GA; Mrs William S. Popham (nee Stoney), Charleston, SC; Carl André Flowers, Cedar Grove Estate, Vicksburg, MS; Creative Caterers, Montgomery, AL; Doris Belcher, Memphis, TN; Ann Dorsey, Full Service Catering, Atlanta, GA; and Mrs John H. Napier III.